Edo D 8/96

STARTING NEEDLECRAFT

Ray Gibson

Edited by Harriet Castor

Designed by Maria Wheatley

Illustrated by Norman Young

Photographs by Ray Moller

Additional photographs by Tony McConnell

Contents

Starting off

This book shows you how to start sewing, and has lots of ideas for things to make.

On these two pages you can see some basic skills you need for all the projects, plus an easy project for you to do right away to try out the techniques.

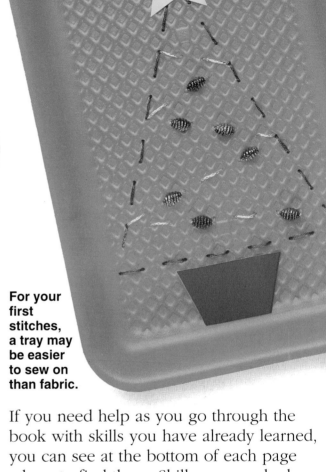

For your first stitches, a tray may be easier to sew on than fabric.

Threading a needle

Threading needles is tricky, so it may take a bit of practice. Hold the needle upright. Push one end of the thread through the hole, or eye.

Try licking and pinching the end of the thread first.

Tying a knot

Thread your needle. Hold the end of the thread in your left hand between finger and thumb. Wind it twice loosely around your finger. Pass the needle under the loops from left to right. Slip the thread off your finger and pull tight.

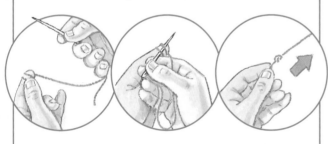

Finishing off

To finish off, do two or three stitches on top of each other. Cut the thread.

Don't pull too tightly.

If you need help as you go through the book with skills you have already learned, you can see at the bottom of each page where to find them. Skills you can look up are written in **bold**.

Here are some of the things you can use in your needlecraft. There is a list of the things you need for the projects on each page. You can find them in department stores or sewing shops.

Christmas tree

Things you need:
A clean polystyrene food tray
Tapestry needle
Embroidery thread
Beads, with holes big enough to pass the needle through
Green pen
Scraps of bright paper

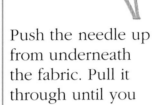

Draw a big triangle on a tray with a green pen.

Make a hole in each corner.

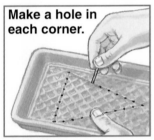

With your needle, poke holes evenly along the lines of the triangle. Thread the needle.

Glue on paper tub shape and star.

Make a knot. Sew in and out of the holes in running stitch. Finish off. Sew beads on inside the shape.

Running stitch

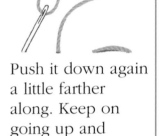

Push the needle up from underneath the fabric. Pull it through until you reach the knot.

Push it down again a little farther along. Keep on going up and down alternately.

Sewing on a bead

If you are in the middle of sewing, put the needle through the bead's hole, and continue.

If you are not, sew over and over on the spot, putting the needle through the bead each time.

Big fish

Things you need:
Paper, 42x30cm (16½x12in)
Two pieces of net, each 42x30cm (16½x12in) (buy net from fabric shops)
Embroidery thread
Scraps of bright paper, fabric and kitchen foil
Needle
Pins

Patterns

A pattern is a paper shape to cut or draw around. You can use patterns again and again.

Draw body only, not fins and tail.

Draw a big fish's body on the paper. Cut it out. This is your pattern.

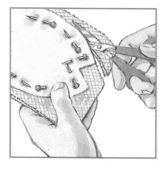

Pin the pattern on one piece of net (see opposite). Cut around the pattern.

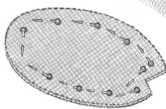

Put pins all around the edge.

Repeat with the other piece of net. Now pin the two net shapes together.

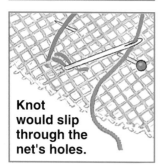

Knot would slip through the net's holes.

Thread your needle. Do not knot the thread. Start with three stitches on the spot instead.

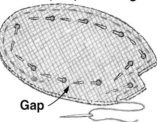

Sew about 1cm (½in) from edge.

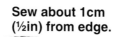

Gap

Sew in **running stitch** around the edge of the fish. Leave a big gap at the bottom.

You could use paper, fabric and foil.

Push lots of scraps through the gap. Sew it up with running stitch. **Finish off**.

To make an eye, glue on a small circle of fabric. You could glue on a sequin, too.

4   **Find out more: Threading a needle - p.2   Running stitch - p.3   Finishing off - p.2**

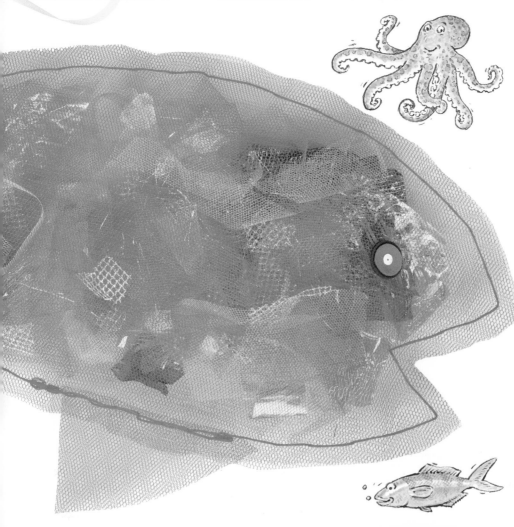

Pins hold things
in place while
you sew.

Push the pin
down through
the layers you
want to join
together.

Push the end of
the pin up
through the fabric
again a little
farther along.

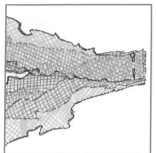

For the tail, cut
some leftover net
into jagged strips.
Pin them together
at one end.

**Take pin out
after sewing.**

Thread the needle.
Sew the tail to the
back end of the
body in running
stitch. Finish off.

To make a fin, cut
out a net triangle.
Pin it onto the
bottom edge of
the body.

Sew the fin on with
running stitch. You
could tie on a loop
of thread to hang
the fish up.

Pom-pom bug

Things you need:
Greaseproof paper
Cardboard, 15x15cm (6x6in)
Two different balls of double knitting yarn
Tapestry needle, small needle, thread and pins
Two pieces of net, each 20x8cm (8x3in)
Scraps of felt
Felt-tip pen
One pipe cleaner
Sequins
Glue

To make a bee, wind all around the ring with black yarn, then yellow, then black again.

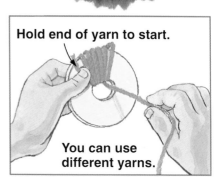

Trace the ring shape on page 29 twice onto greaseproof paper. Glue the paper onto cardboard.

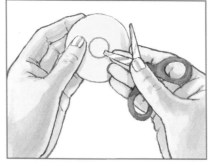

When the glue is dry, cut out the rings. Ask an adult to cut out the middles. Put the two rings together.

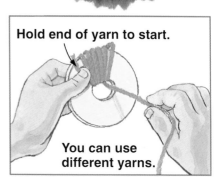

Hold end of yarn to start.

You can use different yarns.

Cut some yarn into long pieces. Wind each around the rings, going through the middle with each wind.

Stop when hole is full.

Keep on winding. When the hole is too small for your fingers, **thread** the yarn onto a tapestry needle.

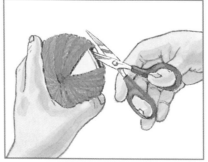

Push some strands apart on the edge of the ring. Poke one blade of some sharp scissors between the rings.

Cut the yarn all the way around, between the rings. If this is too difficult, ask an adult to help you.

Pull the rings apart a little. Wrap a long piece of yarn around in between. Tie it in a tight double knot.

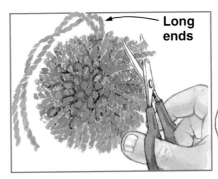

Long ends

Cut off the rings. Fluff out the pom-pom. Snip off uneven ends, except the two long ends in the middle.

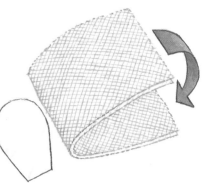

Trace the wing on page 29 onto greaseproof paper. Cut it out. Put the net pieces together. Fold them in half.

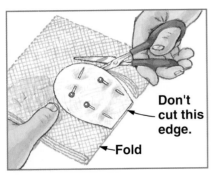

Don't cut this edge.

Fold

Pin the wing shape to the net, with the straight edge along the fold. Cut around the curved edge.

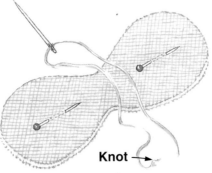

Knot

Remove the pins and paper. Open the net shapes out. Pin them together. Thread a needle and make a **knot**.

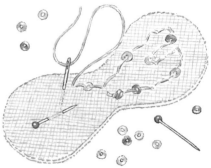

Sew in **running stitch** anywhere you like. Thread sequins on as you go. **Finish off**. Take out the pins.

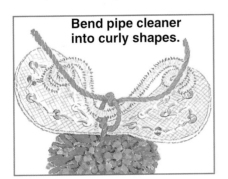

Bend pipe cleaner into curly shapes.

Tie the wings on top of the bug with the long ends of yarn. Bend a pipe cleaner in half and tie it on.

You could add sequins to eyes and nose.

Glue on two felt circles for eyes. Gently pull a piece of yarn in the middle of the face to make a nose.

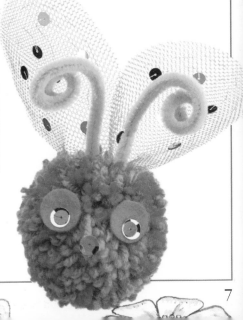

Wizard puppet

Things you need:
Two squares of felt,
22.5x22.5cm (9x9in)
Small pieces of felt - pink,
yellow, white and black
Greaseproof paper
Needle and thread
Black felt-tip pen
Glue

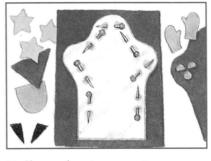

Trace the wizard shapes on page 30 onto greaseproof paper. Cut them out. These are your **patterns**.

Follow the instructions on page 30 for drawing around or pinning the patterns on felt. Cut the felt shapes out.

Tacking tips

Use large **running stitches**. To finish off, do two slanting stitches instead of sewing over and over.

Slanting stitches

To take the tacking out, pull out the thread starting with the last stitch you made. It may help to snip off the knot first.

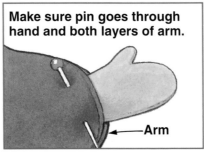

Make sure pin goes through hand and both layers of arm.

Arm

Put the two body shapes together. Slide a hand between the two layers of each arm. **Pin** in place.

Pin rest of body, except the bottom edge. **Thread** a needle. Sew tacking stitches (see left) beside the pins.

Knot

Glove puppet

This is how your hand fits inside the puppet.

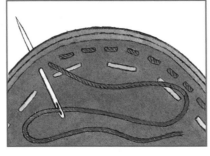

Take out the pins. Sew close to the edge in running stitch. **Finish off**. Take out the tacking.

Dot glue onto the other felt shapes. Press them in place. Look at the big picture to see where to put them.

Glue the beard onto the bottom of the face. Glue the mustache above it.

Mark in the eyes and eyebrows with black felt-tip.

The eyelids are a circle cut in half.

You could glue stars onto the body and the hat.

Glue the feet under the top body piece.

Other puppets

You could make lots of other puppet characters. Use the same pattern for the body, then glue on different shapes.

Dracula puppet

Things you need:
One wooden spoon
Poster paint and brush
20cm (8in) of red ribbon,
1.5cm (¾in) wide
One pearl-top pin (you can use a
small bead threaded on a pin)
Thin black fabric 32x30cm
(12½x12in)
Two pieces of white felt, each
5x5cm (2x2in)
Black felt 7x18cm (3x7in)
One sequin
Black thread for cloak, white
thread for hands
and needle
Greaseproof paper

Paint Dracula's face on the back of the spoon. The back is the side that curves towards you.

Add pearl-top pin for decoration.

Wrap the ribbon around the handle. Tie it in a knot at the front. Tape the ends to the handle.

If fabric has a nicer side, have this on the inside.

Match up the two shorter edges of the thin black fabric. **Pin** together. **Thread** your needle and tie a **knot**.

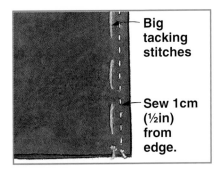
Big tacking stitches

Sew 1cm (½in) from edge.

Tack near pins. Pull pins out. Sew **running stitch** in black thread near the edge. **Finish off**. Pull tacking out.

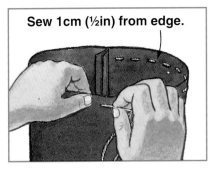
Sew 1cm (½in) from edge.

Turn the fabric the other way out. Sew in small running stitch near one edge. Unthread the needle.

Push fabric along with your fingers.

Loose end

Hold the fabric and pull the loose end of the thread so that the fabric bunches up. This is called gathering.

Leave necktie showing.

Slide spoon handle into the gathers. Pull again so the fabric fits tightly. Re-thread the needle and finish off.

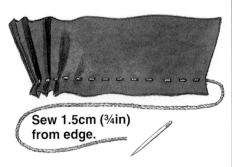
Sew 1.5cm (¾in) from edge.

Sew running stitch in black along one long edge of the black felt. Unthread needle and pull to gather, as before.

Bend corners out.

Fit the felt around the neck. Re-thread needle. Join the edges with small stitches over and over. Cut thread.

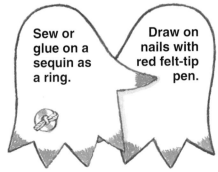
Sew or glue on a sequin as a ring.

Draw on nails with red felt-tip pen.

Trace hand shape on page 28 onto greaseproof paper. Cut out. Draw around it twice on white felt. Cut out.

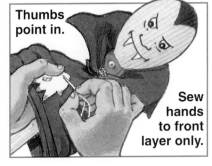
Thumbs point in.

Sew hands to front layer only.

Sew hands onto the front of the body with white thread. Bunch fabric in your hand to get to the right place.

Frog pincushion

Things you need:
Dark green felt 10x11cm
(4x4½in)
Light green felt 16x9cm
(6x3½in)
Yellow felt 1.5x12cm (1x5in)
Thin cardboard 12x12cm
(5x5in)
Greaseproof paper
Needle and
thread
Cotton balls
Felt-tip pen

One shape for lily-pad.

Two shapes for frog.

Trace the shapes on page 28 onto greaseproof paper. Cut them out.

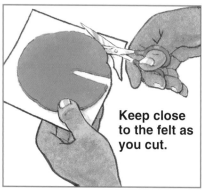

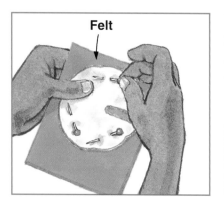

Felt

Pin the lily-pad shape onto the dark green felt. Cut around it. Take out the pins.

Glue the felt shape onto cardboard. When the glue is dry, cut around the felt.

Keep close to the felt as you cut.

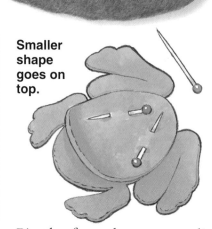

Smaller shape goes on top.

Pin the frog shapes onto light green felt. Cut around them. Pin the felt shapes together.

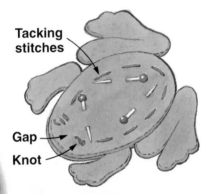

Tacking stitches

Gap

Knot

Thread a needle. Sew near the pins in **tacking** stitches. Leave a big gap at one end.

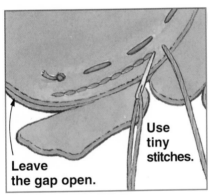

Use tiny stitches.

Leave the gap open.

Take the pins out. Sew close to the edge of the top shape in backstitch (see right).

Backstitch

Make one stitch and bring the needle up to start the next stitch, as for **running stitch**.

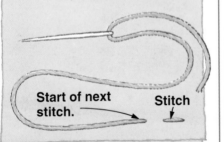

Start of next stitch.

Stitch

Push cotton balls down well.

Finish off. Fill the frog with cotton balls. Sew the gap up in backstitch.

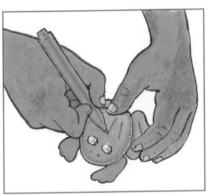

Sew on two **beads** for eyes. Draw on some nostrils and stripes with a felt-tip pen.

Put the needle back into the fabric right by the end of the last stitch.

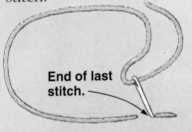

End of last stitch.

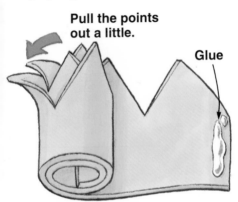

Pull the points out a little.

Glue

Snip one edge of the yellow felt into points. Tightly roll the strip up. Glue end down.

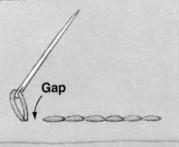

Gently pull up back knees.

Dab glue on underside of feet.

Sit the frog on the lily-pad. Glue the feet down, close to the body. Glue the flower on.

Bring it up again farther on. Make the gap the same size as one stitch.

Gap

Put the needle in where the last stitch ended again. Go on like this.

Pocket mice

Things you need for each mouse:
Pink felt, 15x15cm (6x6in)
Blue felt, 10x5cm (4x2in)
Two tiny two-holed buttons
Cotton balls
Greaseproof paper
Needle, pink thread and black thread
One bead

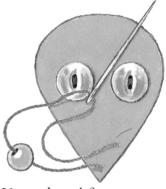

You could make mice of different sizes.

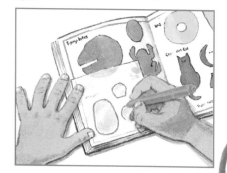

Trace the shapes on page 28 onto greaseproof paper. Cut them out. These are your **patterns**.

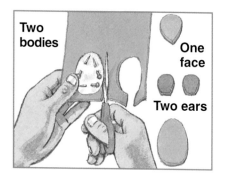

Two bodies

One face

Two ears

Follow the instructions on page 28 for drawing around the patterns on felt. Cut out the shapes.

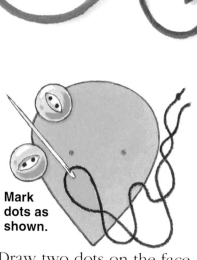

Mark dots as shown.

Draw two dots on the face where the eyes will be. Sew a button on each dot (see right). Use black thread.

Use a bead for a nose. Make several stitches on one spot, passing the needle through the bead on each stitch.

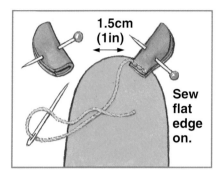

Sew flat edge on.

Fold each ear in half sideways and **pin**. **Tack** the ears to the top of one body piece, 1.5cm (1in) apart.

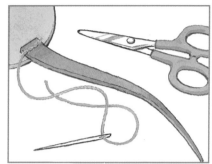

Cut a long, straight pointed tail from blue felt. Sew or glue it on at the bottom of the other body piece.

Sewing on a button

Thread your needle and **knot** the thread. Push the needle up through the fabric, then up through a hole in the button.

Pass the needle down through the button's other hole, then through the fabric. Pull until the button lies flat.

Go back up through the first hole, and down through the second. Do this again. **Finish off** on the back of the fabric.

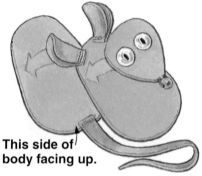

This side of body facing up.

Put the body piece with the ears on top of the body piece with the tail. Put the face on the very top.

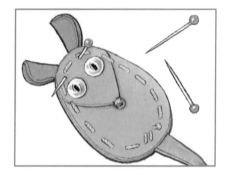

Match up the top edges. Pin the layers together. Thread your needle and tack next to the pins. Take the pins out.

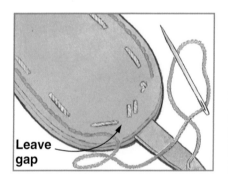

Leave gap

Sew in **backstitch** close to the edge, but leave a big gap at the bottom. Take out the tacking.

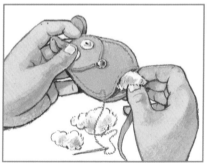

Stuff the body firmly with cotton balls through the gap. Sew the gap up with backstitch. Finish off.

You can wear your mouse in your pocket. Make sure its nose is poking over the top. Its tail could poke out too.

Juggling bags

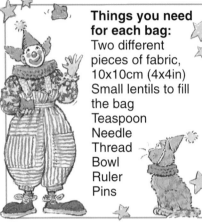

Things you need for each bag:
Two different pieces of fabric, 10x10cm (4x4in)
Small lentils to fill the bag
Teaspoon
Needle
Thread
Bowl
Ruler
Pins

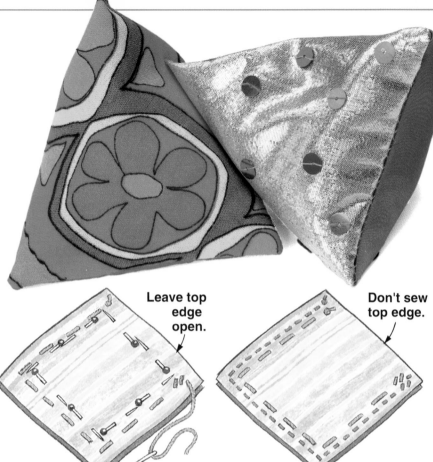

Match up edges.

Brighter side

Knot

Pin the two pieces of fabric, brighter sides together. **Thread** a needle.

Leave top edge open.

Sew **tacking** stitches along three sides of the fabric only. Take out the pins.

Don't sew top edge.

Sew tiny **running stitches** 1cm (½ in) from the edge. **Finish off**. Take tacking out.

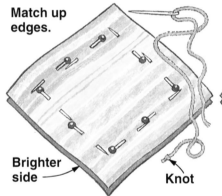

Keeping straight

To keep your sewing straight, cut a square of cardboard 1x1cm (½ x½ in). Use it to check the gap between the edge and your stitches.

Make sure bag is still open.

Turn the top edge outward by 1cm (½ in). Pin, then sew with tacking stitches.

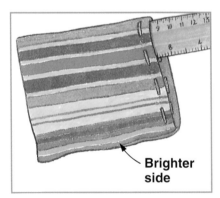

Brighter side

Turn the bag the other way out. Poke the corners out square with a ruler.

Don't fold other square.

Pinch here

Fold top edge of one square in half. Pinch the middle of the edge to start the fold.

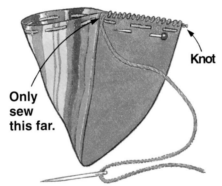

Only sew this far.

Knot

Pin the folded edge. Thread your needle. Sew this edge in oversewing (see right).

Fill the bag about three quarters full.

Take the pin out. Fill the bag with lentils. Hold it over a bowl and use a spoon.

Pinch middle of square as before.

Pin the other half of the top edge. Oversew along it. Take out pins and tacking.

Oversewing

In oversewing, each stitch loops over the edge of the fabric. Hold the fabric flat. Push the needle through it from behind.

Needle comes toward you.

Knot

Pull the thread through. Take the needle back behind the fabric to start the next stitch.

Thread loops over here.

Flying tortoise

Sew three sides of the bag and fill it, as above. Sew up the fourth side as a normal square. Cut out a head, tail and legs from felt. Sew them on.

Draw on a shell pattern with felt-tip pen.

You could sew on sequins.

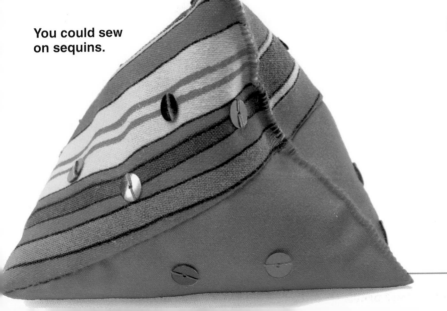

Teddy's sleeping bag

Things you need:
A piece of fabric large enough to wrap around the teddy, with extra space at the bottom and side. Another piece of fabric half as wide as the first, and twice as long as the pillow needs to be.
Needle and thread
Cotton balls
Pins

Hemming

Folded edge

Start with three small stitches on the spot. With the point of the needle, pick up a few threads of the fabric next to the folded edge. Pull the needle through.

Put the needle a little behind the folded edge and push it through toward you. Pull the thread through gently. Pick up a few threads again, and continue.

To make a hot water bottle, cut out two felt shapes. Sew them together, leaving a gap. Stuff them with cotton balls.

Ask an adult to help you measure and cut the fabric to fit your teddy. Cut one piece for the bag and one for the pillow.

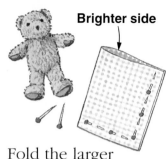

Brighter side

Fold the larger piece in half so it fits around your teddy. **Pin** the long open side and one short side.

Tack near the pins. Take pins out. Sew in **backstitch** or small **running stitch**, 1cm (½in) from the edge.

Finish off. Take out the tacking. Turn the bag the other way out. Poke out the corners with a ruler.

Ask an adult to iron the side seam open at the top, and the top edge down inside by 1cm (½in) all the way around.

Take pins out after tacking.

Turn the top edge down again by 1cm (½in). Pin, then tack near the pins. Hem all around the edge (see left). Finish off.

Leave third edge open.

Brighter side inside.

Take the smaller piece of fabric and put the short edges together. Pin, tack and sew as for the bag.

Turn the fabric inside out. Poke out the corners. Fill the bag with cotton balls. Fold down the open edge by 1cm (½in).

You could decorate the hot water bottle with lines of backstitch.

Take tacking out after sewing.

Pin the layers of this open edge together. Tack near the pins. Take the pins out. **Oversew** along the edge.

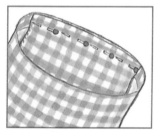

Put the pillow inside the bag. Match up one long side of the pillow with one side of the bag's open edge. Pin together.

Tack near the pins, take them out and oversew along this edge. Take out the tacking. Pull the pillow out of the bag.

Hair scrunchy

Things you need:
Thin, soft fabric, 50x14cm
(19½x5½in)
Needle and thread
15cm (6in) of elastic, 0.5cm
(¼in) wide
Two safety
pins

Brighter side of fabric inside.

Knot

Pin together the shorter
edges of the fabric. **Thread** a
needle. Sew 1cm (½in) from
the edge, in **tacking** stitches.

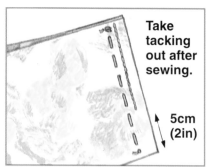

Take
tacking
out after
sewing.

5cm
(2in)

Take the pins out. Sew next
to the tacking in **backstitch**,
starting 5cm (2in) from the
bottom edge. **Finish off**.

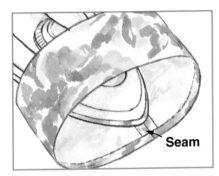

Turn fabric the other way out. Ask an adult to iron the seam flat and the top and bottom edges in by 1cm (½in).

Seam

Turn the top edge down inside so the folded edges meet. Pin them together. Sew in tacking stitches.

←**Folded edges**

Take out the pins. Sew close to the edge in small **running stitch**. Finish off. Take out the tacking.

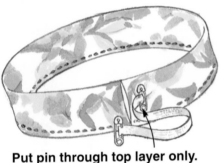

Put pin through top layer only.

Put a safety pin through each end of the elastic. Pin one to the fabric, to the right of the gap.

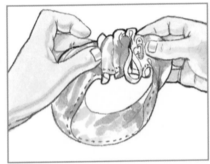

Push the other pin into the gap to the left, as far as it will go. This makes the fabric bunch up.

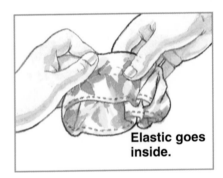

Elastic goes inside.

Hold the pin inside firmly and pull the fabric the other way. Wiggle the pin farther in to the left.

You may need some help.

Continue until the pin gets to the gap again. Keep hold of both ends of the elastic firmly. Take the pins out.

Overlap the ends of the elastic by 2cm (1in). Safety pin together. Sew the edges in oversewing. Take out pin.

Doll's skirt

Sew the shorter sides of a fabric rectangle together. Turn the top edge inward and sew. Thread with elastic as shown above.

Elastic

Tiger needlecase

Things you need:
Orange felt, 15x9cm (6x3½in)
Yellow felt, 15x9cm (6x3½in)
Black felt, 15x9cm (6x3½in)
Black embroidery thread
One small black bead
Black ballpoint pen
Greaseproof paper
White thread
Orange thread
Pins

Trace the tiger shape on page 29 onto greaseproof paper. Cut it out. **Pin** it onto the orange felt.

Cut around the tiger shape carefully. Take the pattern off. Repeat with the yellow and the black felt.

Chain stitch

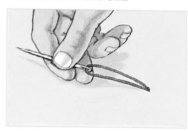

Make a **knot** in your thread. Bring the needle up through the fabric to start the first stitch.

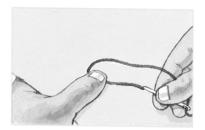

Hold the thread in a loop with your thumb. Put the needle back in right beside where it came out.

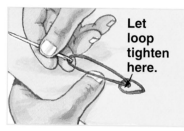

Let loop tighten here.

Bring the needle up again farther on, but inside the loop. Gently pull the thread through.

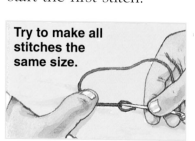

Try to make all stitches the same size.

Put the needle back in near where it came out. Make a loop. Hold it with your thumb and continue.

To finish off, put the needle in just above the last stitch. Pull the thread through to the back.

On the back of the fabric, pass the needle through the last few stitches. Snip the thread.

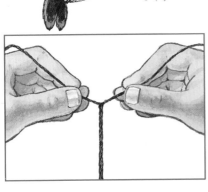

Cut a piece of embroidery thread. Starting at one end, gently pull it apart into two groups of three strands.

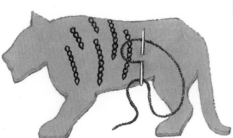
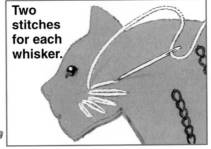

Two stitches for each whisker.

Thread a needle with one group of strands. Sew wavy stripes on the orange tiger in chain stitch (see left).

Sew some short and some longer stripes. Add long white stitches for whiskers. Sew on a **bead** for an eye.

Mark the tiger's mouth very lightly with black ballpoint pen. Mark some dots near the whiskers, too.

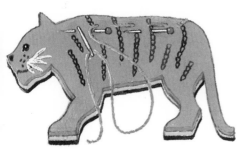
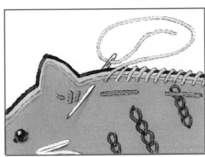

Pin all three tigers exactly together along the top edge. **Tack** near the pins. Take the pins out.

Thread the needle with orange thread. **Oversew** along the top edge, using small stitches. **Finish off**.

Take out the tacking. Open the tigers up like a book, and keep your needles in the middle tiger.

Tying a knot - p.2   Finishing off - p.2   Tacking tips - p.8   Sewing on a bead - p.3   Oversewing - p.17

Cross stitch card

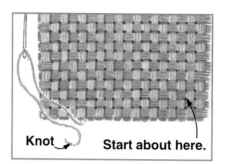

Knot   Start about here.

Start near the bottom right-hand corner of the fabric. Sew a row of 24 cross stitches, with orange thread.

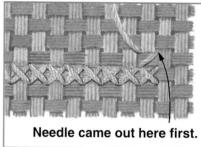

Needle came out here first.

Then bring the needle up through the hole above the one where you started. Sew a new row as before.

Cross stitch

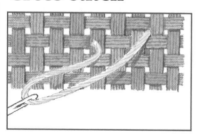

Think of each set of four holes as a square. Pass the needle up through the top right-hand corner hole.

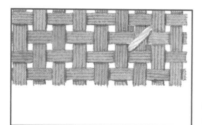

Put the needle down through the hole that is diagonally opposite. This makes a slanting stitch.

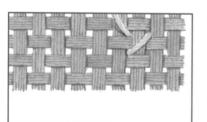

Bring the needle up through the top left-hand hole. Make another stitch the same way. Continue.

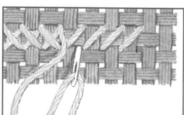

Bring the needle out above the last stitch. Work back the other way. The stitches will cross over.

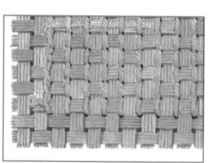

Sew six rows altogether. To finish off, take the needle to the back. Pass it through the last few stitches. Cut thread.

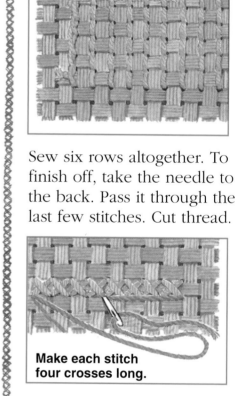

Make each stitch four crosses long.

Thread your needle with red thread. Sew a line of long **backstitch** underneath the cross stitch.

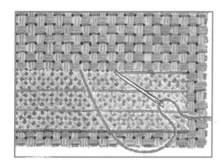

Sew another line after every two rows of cross stitch, until there are four lines altogether.

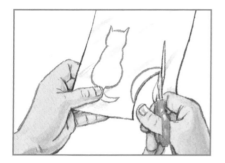

Trace the cat and moon shapes on page 29 onto greaseproof paper. Cut them out.

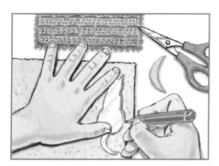

Draw around the cat on grey felt and the moon on yellow. **Pin** them to the felt if they slip. Cut them out.

Put glue on the side you drew on.

Glue on the cat and the moon. With yellow or gold thread, make cross stitches anywhere you like, for stars.

You could glue glitter around the edge.

Trim the fabric to neaten the edges. Fold the cardboard in half and glue the fabric onto the front.

Clown

Things you need:
Cardboard,
12x10cm (5x4in)
Two different
balls of yarn
Felt, 10x17cm
(4x6½in)
Needle and thread
Two tiny beads
for eyes
One larger bead
for a nose
Scissors
Sequins

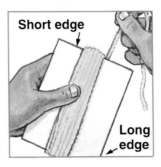

Wind some yarn 20 times around the short edges of the cardboard.

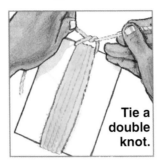

Tie the loops at one end with a piece of yarn. Cut through loops at other end.

Roll a short piece of yarn into a ball. Put it among the strands under the knot.

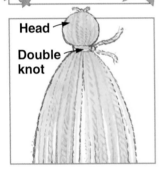

Tie a piece of yarn around the strands below the ball for the neck.

Wind yarn around the long edges of the cardboard 12 times. Tie at each end.

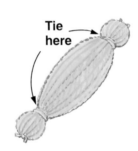

Slide the yarn off the cardboard. Tie a piece of yarn near each end for wrists.

Divide the yarn under the head into two bunches, front and back.

Put the arms in between. Tie some yarn under the arms to make a waist.

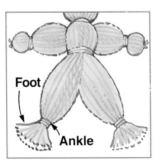

Divide the strands below into two equal bunches. Tie each one near the end.

Trace hat and collar shapes on page 29 onto greaseproof paper. Cut them out.

Pin the shapes onto the felt. Cut around them carefully. Take the pins out.

You could glue on some glitter.

These are clown hats folded over.

You could make hair out of yarn.

For a cloak, gather one edge of a felt rectangle.

Thread a needle. Sew in **running stitch** along one long edge of the collar.

Pull thread to **gather**. Fit collar around neck. Sew over and over at the back to fasten.

You could leave this yarn loose to make a skirt.

You could sew more sequins onto the clown.

Bring needle through from top of head to start.

Glue inside rim.

Sew two small **beads** onto the face for eyes, and one larger one for a nose.

Match up straight sides of hat. **Oversew** them together. Glue it onto the head.

Sewing on a bead - p.3   Oversewing - p.17

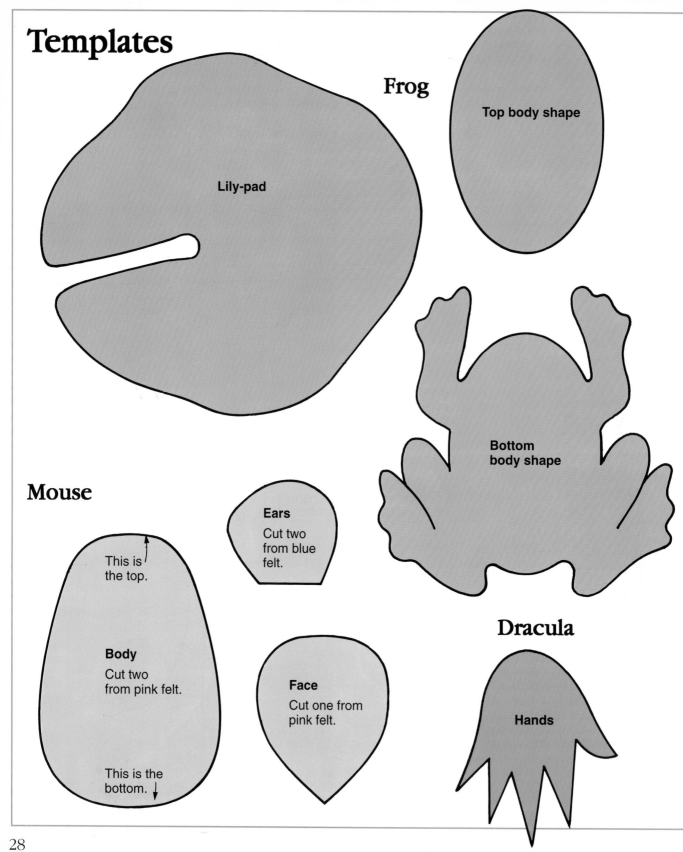

Templates

Frog

Lily-pad

Top body shape

Bottom body shape

Mouse

Ears
Cut two from blue felt.

This is the top.

Body
Cut two from pink felt.

This is the bottom.

Face
Cut one from pink felt.

Dracula

Hands

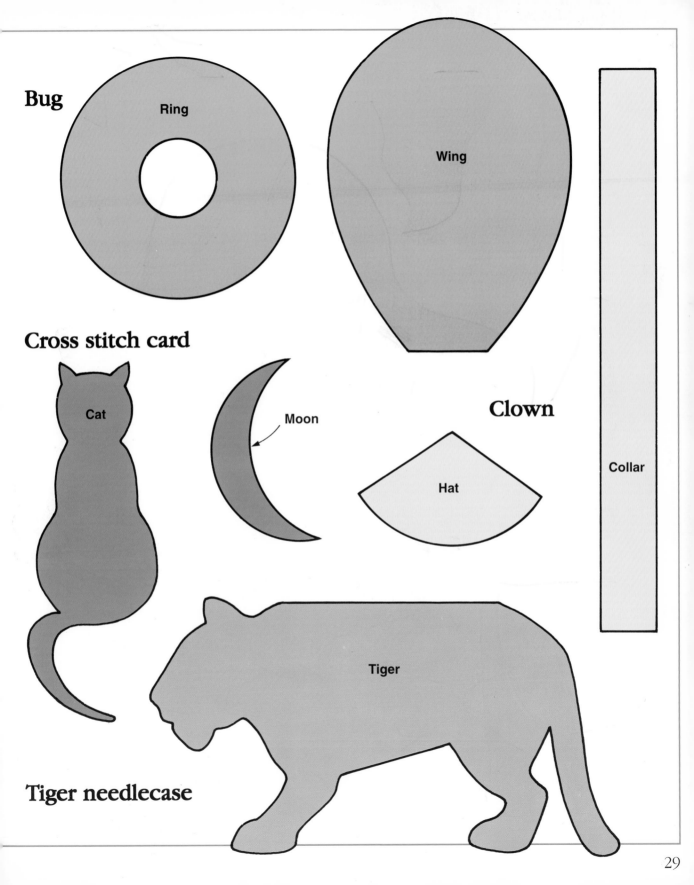

Bug

Ring

Wing

Cross stitch card

Cat

Moon

Clown

Hat

Collar

Tiger

Tiger needlecase

Wizard

Pin the body and hand shapes onto felt and cut around them. Draw around the other patterns, then cut them out.

Beard
Cut one from white felt.

Mustache
Cut one from white felt.

Star
Cut four from yellow felt.

Hands
Cut two from pink felt.

Nose/eyelids
Cut two from pink felt. Cut one of them in half.

Body
Cut two from blue felt.

Hat
Cut one from blue felt.

Face
Cut one from pink felt.

Feet
Cut two from black felt.

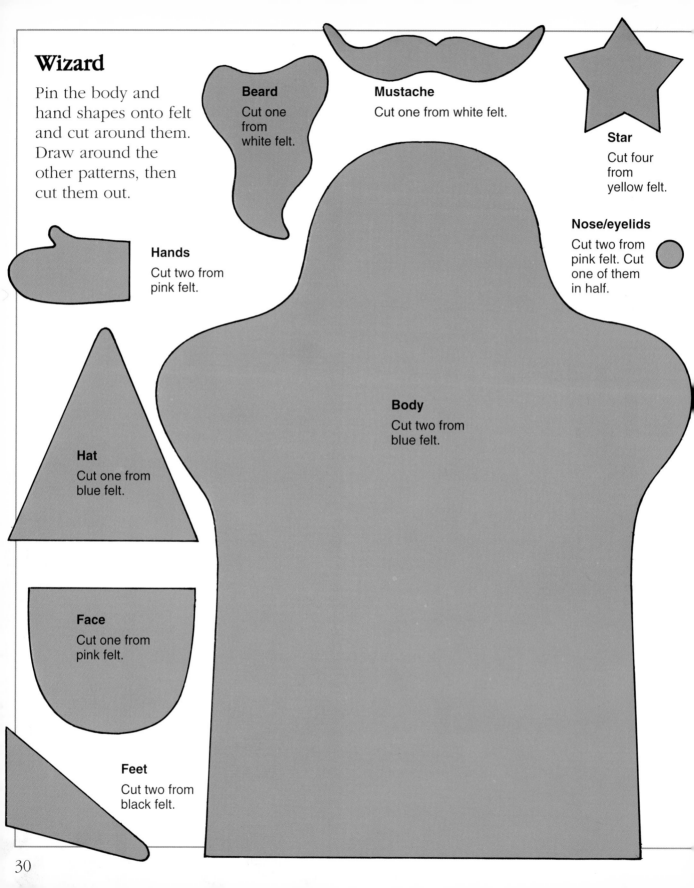

Skills

This page shows you which skills you need for each project in the book. It also shows you where to find out how to do the skills.

The main skills for each project are listed beneath the pictures. Where you learn a skill for the first time, it is shown in **bold**.

Christmas tree

p.2-3 **Threading a needle**; **tying a knot**; **finishing off**; **running stitch**; **sewing on a bead**.

Big fish

p.4-5 **Using patterns**; **pinning**; running stitch.

Pom-pom bug

p.6-7 **Making pom-poms**; using patterns; pinning; running stitch.

Wizard puppet

p.8-9 Using patterns; pinning; **tacking**; running stitch.

Dracula puppet

p.10-11 Pinning; tacking; running stitch; **gathering**; using patterns.

Frog pincushion

p.12-13 Using patterns; pinning; tacking; **backstitch**; sewing on a bead.

Pocket mice

p.14-15 Using patterns; **sewing on a button**; sewing on a bead; pinning; tacking; backstitch.

Juggling bags

p.16-17 Pinning; tacking; running stitch; **oversewing**.

Sleeping bag

p.18-19 Pinning; tacking; backstitch or running stitch; **hemming**; oversewing.

Hair scrunchy

p.20-21 Pinning; tacking; backstitch; running stitch; **threading elastic**.

Tiger needlecase

p.22-23 Using patterns; **chain stitch**; pinning; tacking; oversewing; sewing on a bead.

Cross stitch card

p.24-25 **Cross stitch**; backstitch; using patterns.

Clown

p.26-27 Using patterns; running stitch; gathering; sewing on a bead; oversewing.

Helpful hints

Here is a reminder of the stitches you have learned in this book, and what they are best used for. There are some helpful hints on the equipment you need for the projects, too. You should be able to find everything in department stores or sewing shops.

Stitches

Backstitch - this is a strong stitch that makes a continuous line on the fabric. To start each new stitch, the needle goes back to the end of the last.

Chain stitch - usually, this is just for decoration. The stitches make loops that look like links in a chain.

Cross stitch - this stitch is usually for decoration, too. Each stitch makes the shape of a cross.

Hemming - this stitch is used when the edge of a fabric needs to be turned in so it does not fray (unravel). The stitching is done on the inside, so that as little as possible will show.

Oversewing - here, each stitch loops over the edge of the fabric.

Running stitch - this is a simple stitch, with stitches spaced at regular intervals.

Tacking - this is like running stitch, but larger. It holds pieces of fabric together while you sew them properly. Then it is taken out.

Equipment

Binca or Aida - a type of fabric with large, regular holes suitable for cross stitch.

Beads - make sure you choose beads with holes that are big enough to pass the needle through.

Embroidery thread - the type used in this book is stranded cotton, made of six strands twisted together.

Glue - always use a water-based glue.

Needles - unless told otherwise, use small needles suitable for sewing with ordinary sewing thread.

Tapestry needles - these are large needles with blunt ends. They are suitable for sewing with thicker types of thread.

Left-handed sewing

The illustrations in this book show right-handed sewing. The sewing in every case can be done from left to right instead. It may help left-handed readers to hold a mirror up to the illustrations.

With special thanks to Hannah Watts, who appears on page 20.

First published in 1994 by Usborne Publishing Ltd, Usborne House, 83-85 Saffron Hill, London EC1N 8RT, England. Copyright © 1994 Usborne Publishing Ltd. First published in America in August 1994. AE.